Mab Jones

take your experience
and peel it

Indigo Dreams Publishing

First Edition: take your experience and peel it
First published in Great Britain in 2016 by:
Indigo Dreams Publishing
24, Forest Houses
Cookworthy Moor
Halwill
Beaworthy
Devon
EX21 5UU

www.indigodreams.co.uk

Mab Jones has asserted her right under the Copyright, Designs
and Patents Act 1988 to be identified as the author of this work.
© Mab Jones 2016

ISBN 978-1-910834-20-6

British Library Cataloguing in Publication Data. A CIP record
for this book can be obtained from the British Library.

Designed and typeset in Palatino Linotype by Indigo Dreams.
Cover design by Ronnie Goodyer from artwork by Fran
Williams.
Printed and bound in Great Britain by 4edge Ltd.

Papers used by Indigo Dreams are recyclable products made
from wood grown in sustainable forests following the guidance
of the Forest Stewardship Council.

I dedicate this book to the powers of change and transformation;

to the light which resides within every one of us;

and to J.G.

Thanks to J.G. for his love and support, and for being the subject matter of several of these poems. Thanks, after that, to Arts Council Wales for the gift of a Creative Wales Award which allowed me time and space to learn and study, to attend the Poetry Masterclass at Ty Newydd, and so to write some of these pieces; and to Literature Wales for their continuing support. Thank you to the National Botanic Garden of Wales for allowing me to be their Resident Poet for three years, which resulted in some of these poems; to Artes Mundi for commissioning me to respond to work; to photographer Dan Green for asking me to write poems for the graffiti project on Cranbrook Street, Cardiff; to the Dylan Thomas Boathouse where I worked on a couple of these when I was Resident Poet for 2 months in 2015.

Some of these poems have appeared in other places: 'Birth', and 'When' were published in Nutshells and Nuggets; 'Black Sheep' was published on i am not a silent poet; 'Lover' was published in Picaroon Poetry; 'Poem in Which Canned Laughter is Returned' was a winner in the Live Canon International Poetry Competition 2015 and published in their winners' anthology; 'I was a boy' and 'these bones' are currently on a wall in Cranbrook Street, Cardiff; the haiku I've called 'Roath Park' was published in the Japanese newspaper, The Mainichi; the other haiku in that series were printed on a tote bag for the Made In Roath Festival in Cardiff; 'Styx' was published in the anthology From The Roaring Deep (Biblioteca Alexandrina, 2015); 'Selene' was published in the anthology Lunessence (Biblioteca Alexandrina, 2016); 'Ascension' was published both in The Western Mail and in The Stare's Nest. Many thanks to all of these for the publications.

Also by Mab Jones:

Poor Queen (Burning Eye Books, 2014)
10 of the Best (Parthian, 2011)

CONTENTS

take your experience
and peel it

Pulp Fiction

Take your experience
and peel it. Pull back the skin
and drop it to the floor
like a skirt.

Next, the pulp,
firm and glistening as a heart.
Crush it.

Finally, find the pips,
as smooth and honest
as bullets. Swallow them,
like medicine.

Writer, you are ready.

Begin.

Birth

When the tectonic plates of my skull
Were squeezed through that canal,
And I slipped into the world
Like a creature from its shell,

A cry ballooned inside me
And escaped from my small body,
A raw and wrinkled pink thing
Sinking swiftly through dark water.

Bracelet

I found you again the other day
and almost threw you out – mistook
you for a withered rubber band;
a rotting, disc-shaped crisp.

Brown and thin and dull as
my remembrance, I plucked you from
the box and went to fling you
into the black bag, gaping, mouth-ike.

My fingers, feeling your coldness,
paused, and pulled you closer,
recognition shining at your shape.

You were once a fairy thing,
a pretty curse, a copper circlet
clasped upon my tiny
toddler's wrist.

Now, I fit three fingers in.
You are as light as a twig.
Powerless, and dull.

I cannot remember that wide-eyed
child, so pretty and unspeaking;
her head bent under a weight of curls,
this bracelet heavy, biting.

Inheritance

Mother, the last I heard from you
you were married to a man who took
all your money and gambled it away;
your spine crumbling to nothing;
your sciatic nerve still jittering its
syllables like a stitched-up lip.

Your whole life so far, mum,
has been like a Chinese finger trap.
You have accepted its biaxial braid
more than you do your own DNA.
That shrinking circumference
your most familiar embrace, these days,

replacing the pinning limbs of men;
their fish hook promises and weighted
rings. Existence for you is a choking thing,
tightening and shrinking as you writhe;
and so you try not to, mouthing like
a fish when bad news arrives but still

letting it in. Your front door always
open; your mouth turned upwards
like a scythe. Mother, you are smiling,
but I can hear the sighs beneath
as your heart itself is squeezed,
as your arteries strangle themselves,

as your bones knit themselves thin
in order to accommodate the tiny
life you find yourself within. The ties
that tighten a net you cast yourself –
glistening at your neck, bound around
your baby daughter's wrist.

The Night Ship

A ship sailed into my head one night –
unfolded its sails within my brain,
unfurled its flag, and sat there in the calm
blue ocean of my imagination, waiting.

I don't know what it came for, what
it holds. Its cargo might be silver, gold,
silk or coal; mangoes from far distant
groves, or the glistening bodies of slaves.

It might be a ghost ship, sailors dead.
Its white plumage like a monstrous bird.
Is it anchored? I don't know. Perhaps
it's casting nets which I can't see,

perhaps it's fishing for a thing I own,
a treasure from within my mental deeps.
My worry is it might be holding words,
my neck too slim to let them out through speech.

Gold

My colour is gold, beginning with the too-
bright, brassy breast-chains of my mother,

Argos-bought and brilliantine, as if a child's
imitation of that rare and precious metal;

wound like slender snakes around her, pendants
resting between bosoms over-tanned, too-bare

but for these; ordered for birthdays and Christmas,
which were the same, for her; fourth born on that day

so the light of her name never reached the paper;
first born in a family where only milk bottle tops shone,

medallions made for the mouths of richer children, all
that milk and cream and cwtch she never got to sip.

For me, the colour sifts to something here inside
the bosom, not listed in the gloss of a catalogue;

a thing which can't be bought or sold, but only found;
all the easier, somehow, when your mother never could.

1969

Why only a summer of love,
if love is infinite and everlasting?

Why not an autumn, a winter,
a spring of clutching kissing blossoms

full to bursting with joy?
Was the revolution we were promised

merely spin, a snake swallowing
its own tail with addict urgency?

When a man put his foot
on the cold body of a moon,

and my father put his hand
on the warm body of my mother,

was there any need to mark
that territory with a ring, or flag?

Red for the blood of a maidenhead taken,
blue for the sadness of summer's end ...

What is this need to quantify love,
yet dare to declare it as free?

Black Sheep

I was a white sheep once, but sullied.
Hard to say now, with my soot-black back
if I was ever really clean. Black sheep
of a flock who never really stopped to ask
why I rarely, if ever, went *baa*.

Now, happiness has gathered them
in at their pen: a contentment hooked
on a crook's lies, and set in a bed of
biting tics. I watch from the edge of a field,
unable to run, or bleat.

My dark wool thick with fear, shame;
the pain of a lullaby childhood ripped away.
Are you all getting along these days?
Has the past been tethered to its post
and left to scream?

Memories come like animal mouths to pinch me
awake. Blood once again seeps to soil my thighs.
A raincloud heavy as a body is pressing the sky,
thickening like a blanket, getting ready
to release its load.

Geometry

My girl's grey eye was gradient-
lined, the sides of the sharp isosceles
spearing, as I sat in my seat
like a lost pocket toffee, and sweated
while sums made their endless
demands. No end or beginning

to that fairy tale jail, where the witch,
old Miss Withey, crooked her chalk-
cracked hands and fossilised fingers,
hooked at my collar, picked my pink
brain; her dew-dreamed youth lost,
consumed by protractors; ruler'd, cruelly,

away. And I was a princess who pricked
her thick finger on a compass's needle
and slept: my mind's eye then dreaming
the lid of my desk as a long forgot
trapdoor to Narnia. I was Mrs Tumnus.
I nicked the Snow Queen's coat. My eyes

became soap bubbles, bigger than Bambi's –
I did not need to wear glasses. There,
my specs expanded into a castle's crazy
arches, my uniform's stripes broke free;
the fractions' evil curse was killed; my
animal self could speak.

Some Things I Have Been

I have been a doormat,
a footstool – a thing to
wipe your feet on, rest your
toes. And I have been
a comfy chair, a waiting
seat, a throne to any passing
fool (frog bodies squatting on
me, my arms and legs their home).
And I have been a bed
at times, a soft and silky
place; a sanctuary of pillows
soothing salivating heads.
A lampshade and a bathtub,
a cupboard or a shelf. Come
kiss me and caress me,
and I would be a thing
for you. I would be that thing
you call a woman.

Sunflower

You came to us a seed – a single, striped
pellet plummeting to earth; spinning like a
tumbler; landing, with literal pot luck, in soil
we had set aside for a smaller sort of flower.

We thought you were a weed, at first, but
wondered, and waited; watched your neck
unfurling like a viper; your fists un-bunching,
your head punching up. Green and juicy,

the colour of a jungle, you were incongruent
amongst our daffodils and pansies, the neatly
plotted rows of shrubs. Finally, you flowered,
and put my marigolds to shame with your

flame-yellow petals. Of course you are a miracle –
braving the beak or belly of a bird, then
falling through the clouds. It's a courage
I have never known, a blindness I would not

dare. I need to know where I am going.
I have my narrative, which is as unlike yours
as you are from the pale geraniums; from my
marigolds, up here, pacing inside the sink.

Blodeuwedd

Written for a performance with Artes Mundi in 2014, inspired by the work of Ragnar Kjartansson and Sanja Iveković in Ffotogallery.

Once there was a perfect woman,
a woman made of flowers.
No lips, but a single budding violet
in semblance as if to speak.
No eyes but shining buttercups
reflecting the sun on throats.
A muted woman with a neck of stems,
swollen with sap, soundless.
Naked one could see her skin
was composed of soft, pink roses,
velvet-smooth and blushing,
made for smelling and smoothing,
asking to be plucked.
Her arms and legs were hyacinths,
perfuming the air with scent,
ready as if for embrace. Yes,
there was a perfect woman,
once. No sex parts to speak of
for every inch of her was blooming,
a thousand flower mouths open,
so many orifices waiting, asking
to be entered by tongues and fingers.
She could be smelled for miles and
miles, her pollen pulled people
from their mundane lives into her
shining, petalled presence. The only
perfect woman to ever have existed,
she stood rooted to the spot.

Puya

Written for the puya chilensis, which bloomed for the first time in 10 years at the National Botanic Garden of Wales in 2012. The plant possesses spiked leaves which hook in small creatures and then feed from their blood; however, when it isin bloom, its flowers are full of a sweet nectar which animals and even humans can drink.

Puya, they call you. The word sticky
in their mouths. You prickle the roof
of the glass house, unsettle the groups
of visiting classes. Like a nettle, your
leaves are stingsharp, laced with thorns.
"Cruel", they remark. Your taste is for
animal flesh, which they hook, pull in, and
starve to death. Their blood is your food.

Your bed more wet with this than dew.
From the Andes to Llanarthney you
came. A monster baby in a way: eight
feet tall and closer to a mutant than
a flower. Towering above the others,
a giant in the nursery. Cursed to slowness,
reliant on your new owners, still you
grew, your brontosaurus neck too thick
for them to prune; a Chilean imposter
that loomed above its human masters.

But now, a decade later, you're in bud,
about to blossom. Your body as round
and fulsome as a woman's. Crowds
come to marvel, wondering at your
beauty. Eyes hunger for your form.
Cameras snap and looks are thrown,
but sweeter than before. You ignore
them; take no note. Your name now
sweet as nectar in every thirsting throat.

Imperial

Written for Welsh Wildflower Day, after a talk in the National Botanic Garden of Wales.

I am trying to find the beauty in you, buttercup.
I am looking only at your golden heads.
I am attempting to forget what the expert said:
that your species is invasive.
That your style is 'creeping'.
That your taste is acrid.
That your sap can cause blistering.
You carry your poison so prettily,
you are lovely to behold, intermingled
with the daisies, as if you were one of them.
As if you could ever be 'common'.
You will live for a thousand years
and gradually those daisies will be crowded out.
You will block the light from them, put them in the shade,
steal the soil's potassium from beneath their roots,
secrete toxic chemicals from your own that
they will drink, unknowingly.
Thinking that you are a friend.
They will feed it to their children and their children
will become weak. You will smile as their heads grow limp,
as each generation is born smaller, feebler.
One day, there won't be any births at all.
And still the passers-by will look at you,
and marvel at your pretty golden heads,
so many of them, like cups, reflecting the sunlight
from above, so beautiful, full only of themselves.
The soil beneath now richer than it ever was.

Poortistic

Once I attempted towards a politeness
which I, as a pauper, had never been taught.
Table manners, what were these?
I learned to use my knife and fork
on my knees, in the wrong hands,
skewiff, like diggers. No napkins, no croutons,
no dessert spoons, no prayers.

Poortistic, I knew not punctilious, I was punk
without ever intending it: spat when I spoke,
smeared snot on sleeves, barked, howled, stole,
and lied. Please and thankyou, I did not know.
I shook in response or stared – silent – a stone
as yet un-thrown.

Later, I learned the ways
of the posh girls who sang their prayers
while I sniffed. Used tissues, hair brush, lip balm,
bra. Said thank you, bless you, please and ta,
so unlike I, who was without religion, or regret.

Their pony hair alongside my mullet-mess.
Their sunfreckles next to my mole.

These days I do repartee,
peppermill, hankie, spelt. Drape my meatself
with pearls as white as phlegm. Earrings like
drips of spit. Wear florals, spritz on scent...

...but still, beneath, my hackles rise, my
pink maw opens woundlike. Still I howl, from time
to time, my manicured, moisturised,
sunkissed, ringdressed fingers
pistolling up.

Lover

Written after a visit to Llandough Psychiatric Unit.

Your mind, like blown glass,
has cracked.

They have taped up
what they can. Only a few
fragments are missing.

In the tea room,
an older woman in tight jeans brags about how
you give her bear hugs.

In the hallway, a girl
is pulling herself toward the door,
on the floor. Ragdoll thin,
her hair streams behind her
like a wedding veil.

You are bearded. A young prince.
Dandruff confettis your shoulders
as you hold court.

You are popular here.
It is Sunday, and I am your fifth visitor.

You tell me you love me.
You want to show me your poems but
they are in the older woman's room.

I see two people I know:
a sex offender I taught to write haiku;
a well-to-do woman
I need to invoice for work.

You put sugar in my coffee,
forgetting that I do not
take it.

You kiss me. I kiss back.
I am let out and walk past traffic,
keep walking until
I don't know where I am.

You drink tea. Set up pieces
on a board game
you do not know how to play.

Paper Man

At first, paper man,
I admired your cutting edge,
your inability to be anything more than
see-through. I noticed you
folding in certain situations.
I thought it was your nature.
I watched you crumple,
poor screwed-up you,
and I cried and cried.
You had been punched, and
you had been burned, and
I could see so many holes.
The thought of flames hurting
you, hurt me even more.
But then I saw you taking the match
to yourself, and I did not
understand it. Tried to stop it, in fact.
But you would find those matches
wherever they were hidden.
I told you it was over, and you
posted yourself to me in an envelope.
Love me, you'd written on the place
where your heart should have been.
Hate me, was written over your pencilled cock.
I crumpled you into a ball
and threw you from the window, but still
you returned – masquerading as a
bill, a letter, a Christmas card,
an origami swan. And every time
I let you in – the fire, the smoke,
filled my flat and my lungs. Licked at
my heart. Paper man, I am tired of this.
The water I throw just turns you to mulch,

my pleas to stop are ignored.
I finally see that you don't have ears.
You don't have a heart, either.
You are so thin, now,
and you are just paper,
but still you left me in cuts all over
while I in turn have changed to other
things. Water. Wood.
Finally, to stone.

What She Made

Mother's milk is fed to the baby
to make it grow, to feed its muscles,
to strengthen, lengthen bones. From her
heart and through her breasts, it drips –
carrying antibodies, carrying vitamins,
carrying everything baby needs to
grow up big and strong. She feeds it
to him, tit in mouth; cooing, soothing.
the baby, still unseeing, sucking
down her body's liquid. Cell of her cells,
blind to all, he is safe within her arms.

He is safe, within her house, within
the bedroom, like a cell. His body and
his brain are built, can only be undone
in ways that we all know: the window
in the beer glass base; that doorway
shaped by smoke. And through it all
her ringing, clinging: when will I see you?
I need to, I need you, you can't spend
all your time with *her*. The milk now sour but
he drinks down. It feeds him, feeds what's in him.
What she put there. What she made.

Poem in Which Canned Laughter is Returned

Finally, we thought to give them back; return them
to their makers; the bellies they'd tumbled out of, years ago;
the owners of the lips they'd danced from, juicy as
tomatoes, round and fat and fearless.

Into the wide-thighed lap of a waitress we gently
set her guffaw, progeny of a comedy skit she'd witnessed
years ago. Childless, she was grateful, the return
of the forgotten merriment a salve to her wrinkling ova.

From that same can a titter, sluiced from the
oesophagus of a now much older man, once thin-hipped;
long-haired. He accepted the giggle with an embarrassed
air, his chortles these days were richer, meaty, stout

with a sense of importance. They exploded
from his fauces with forceful, fist-like aplomb. This
underfed snigger irked the man, but he took it in
like a son; like a bastard, with grudging acceptance.

One old lady refused the return. She could not remember
laughing so hard, so large. Sighed like a needle
when she saw it; shook her purple hair like an ancient
swab of lavender. This lively chuckle, kicking up
from beneath heaving breasts, could not be hers.

In the end, we took it away; released it, later, into the
city, where sometimes it snuck up upon other elderly ladies
and took them, for a moment, by force. Wiping their tears
away after, the women would tremble, and wonder.

For many of the canned inhabitants, of course,
there was no reunion, or release. They'd grown used
to their small metallic world. Like circus lions they knew
no other way. The sound they made was still loud enough,

but it was a performance, now, not a freeing of tension;
not a bubble of pent-up pressure, released. Each rendition
was exactly the same and, once it was complete, they would
climb back into their aluminium hut, and lie down, wearily;
waiting to be called upon, again.

I was a boy

For Ernest Willows, the Cardiff airship pioneer.

I was a boy, with a boy's
enthusiasm for flight –
things with wings and, later on,
balloons. At nineteen I exchanged
dentistry for dirigibles, the tombstone
rows of neat teeth for clouds.
Cumulus. Nimbostratus. Cirrus.
I repeated their names like a mantra
as I stitched the ribs of my first ship.
Finally, I rose, imagination's bubble
made rubber, gas, and metal.
Swami-like I swam through air, circling
the Eiffel Tower as a bumblebee
does a flower. Sometimes I dream
that I am sinking, my ship's skin alight,
and I am burning, trailing a tail
of flame as I fall. But then I wake and
I am a boy again, with a boy's
idealism, innocence, and passion,
my airship still to be dreamt, then built;
imagination yet to spark, ignite.

Ghost

With all the many devils wrestled
from your frame; battled from your
bones; plucked from you like biting
tics, leaving tooth marks in their
wake; your young skin mottled from
that horde, the lipless mouths of

demon drink and druggish urge:
how can I complain about the slender
wraith that's left there now, wisping
round your ribs; sliding from inside
your lungs, the space you hold below
your heart and let out through your lips?

The spectre left within you is thin:
not a muscled monster, as before.
Fragrant, mist-like, it might be an
aftershave, or scent: except we know
that one day it could kill. I suck it in –
this smoke, this urge to tell you no.

We walk together, draped in
lethal fumes. It is a blanket,
smothering us both; a bedsheet
round our necks. A ghost we share,
its fingers in our throats; an apparition,
winding round our heads.

Stabiliser

That white paper, wafer-thin,
names the thing the doctor says
will help with recent moods.

I've been up and down like a yo-yo.
A simile you used to smile at,
before that toy went wild and wound you

up within its string. Now, whims
fill you, make you giggle one minute, clutch
razors in your palm the next, sweet

silverfish which you let nip and
slice at skin. Red graffiti marks
your palms, veins jump, rope-like,

from your wrists. I ask
what's been prescribed but you can't
read the doctor's hand.

It begins with a Q, you tell me,
ends with the word 'line'. I suggest a name
and you're hysterical –

It sounds like a kind of eastern dance!
I don't know how you'd know.
You hopscotch to the next topic,

girlish despite your age, trusting
the prescription with its curling, looping
pen, the pill you cannot name.

These Bones

A poem inspired by Cathays in Cardiff, which was home to the UK's first recorded mosque, as well as one of the country's largest Victorian cemeteries.

Laid out on earth, or just below;
clothed in flesh, or dressed in soil;
these bones circled once-same souls,
their humming hearts and lungs
which sang the salat or the psalm.

Beneath a crescent moon or cross;
on woven thread or in a box of polished
wood, these bones once held the selves
of those who stepped here once,
who laughed and dreamed like us.

In hijab or in Sunday best;
arms straight or folded at the chest,
these bones enclosed the minds and hearts
of those who prayed, were laid to rest
right here, are near and yet so far –

in history, in memory; this city, these bones
which cradled our parents; who cradled our own.

Cardiff Haiku

Elm Street

Sugar pink, baby
blue – sweet dreams, maybe, behind
the lidded windows

City Road

Silken dresses hang
on display, like promises
waiting to be kept

Wellfield Road

Well-to-do woman
drops two pennies on the ground –
her final purchase

Albany Road

Shopping in one hand,
child in the other – a list
of things still to do

Roath Park

Young girl running,
her hair like a comet –
darkness after

Flood

Written in the Hunterian Museum, Royal College of Surgeons, London.

This is the ark
with half its inhabitants
missing; the animals
entering one by one,
and asked to remove
their coats at the door.

Only the ugliest have
been invited – the rare,
the strange; those
robed in disease, or
draped in polyps.

Here, the imperfect are
grouped like superheroes:

a duck with four legs;
a foetal calf, its mandible
eating its own maxilla;
a faceless puppy
wrinkling its existence
from inside a tube.

Elsewhere, the spinal cord
of a minke whale
reminds me of a bell rope.

A mammary reservoir
is pinned and splayed
like a treasure map.

The tongue of a wildebeest:
a hitch-hiker's thumb.

Finally I come
to the unbirthed babies.

Suspended in liquid,
small face serious,
this one is Confucius.
This one is an alien.
This one is carved from soap.

Somewhere inside me
a tide is rising. Brain
flooded with images
I leave the museum,

imagination stranded
on a higher peak.

Styx

I swore upon your river, once. Obsidian ribbon
at my feet. Your waters silent witness to my vow.

Older than the gods, you heard. Took my words
and held them tight. Dirt that might produce a pearl,

if I kept my pledge. I trembled as I spoke to you,
my face reflected in your strait as if it was a mirror,

made of oil or ink. My own eyes formed of onyx.
I imagined they were yours. Stone-hard, set in white,

the parchment of my face; the mouth my autograph,
lips as thin as a snake's. Later on, you learned I'd lied,

though I think you always knew. Your slim arms
winding round me. My breath, withering fast.

Aqueous

Inspired by wild swimmer and artist Natasha Brooks

The human woman peels away the layers.
Jacket. Gender. Jumper. Class. Something
like an onion, slipping loose of skins;
the stitches of each drape, dissolving;
identity itself unfastened, shimmied out of
like a skirt and left at the side of the lake.

Having shed these skins, then, the human
woman dives, into the earth's blue eye,
as numinous as milk. The swaddling dark is
soothing, makes of her an infant; croons her
to a baby; sings her from her cradling bones;
hymns her to an atom. In the un-sun, star-less

dark, she is herself no more. Eventually, naked
spark, she rises; regains what was shriven;
identity's cloak enfolding what was freed.
Patella jewelled with salt; beads of fluid at her
neck, she surges back to being. Reborn, the
human woman stands, and learns herself again.

In Praise of Bodies, Celestial and Otherwise

Astronomical bodies relax into rounded shapes –
see the planets, as example. No oblongs, cubes, or
rhomboids, there. Nothing annoyingly pointed; no
cone-style spikes, à la Madonna, or those Cornetto-esque
contraptions 50s starlets squashed themselves into.
The universe does not wear a bra. The universe

hangs loose, jiggles joyfully; accepts its comets, its asteroids; the
wormholes, inflating one minute, collapsing again the next. It
doesn't hold itself in. It is ever-expanding. Don't tie yourself
into corsets, love, but look to the cosmos as a paradigm.
Mercury's wrinkles and Mars's flushed complexion mark them
as unique. Your beauty spots and

freckles, that patch of eczema which erupts now and then,
are just as wondrous, and wonderful. You might say
that Jupiter is big, but look at all its moons! 63 at the last count.
It takes a certain kind of body to draw that level of audience; to
keep so many attendant. Don't worry about your lumpy bits –
your mass look great to me, and I notice

other people observing it, too. It's what pulled me into your
orbit, at first, before I discovered your hidden depths, swathed
beneath your cloud-like cardigans, your specs; your
introverted-yet-pleasant demeanour below that
cool, calm shell. Some think you're as icy as Io, but really
you are a star; older, but remember, too, that stellar

remnants shine as brightly as new-born suns. That's why I'm
your satellite; the Luna to your Terra. I circle you with my
arms, measure days by each rotation. And, though they say it's
dangerous, you compel my naked eye. And though they warn
of solar flares, you're the one I always return to.

Selene

Sometimes the moon is round; sometimes
she is as slender as a bone. Sometimes she
rolls across the sky, her marble beauty swathed
in silken cloud; at other times her roundness

wanes, her hips are hooks with which she
spears her way. Selene, you teach us not to
hate our form, we women who grow plump,
then thin, then fat; to love our chubby arms,

our skinny limbs, our bodies which are fulsome,
and then not. And so we have our lovers, same
as you: our youthful boys, with curling hair,
smooth backs; their muscles wrapped around us,

lips entwined, and all our dimples lose their
shyness at his hand. Like you, our body's
changeable, fallible, and stark; illuminating
darkness as we follow in your path.

Rainbow

For you, I'd kill a rainbow. Set treasure
in a field, and wait. And when the creature

came to feast, I'd let the trap snap shut;
work to drag that thrashing arch back home.

For you, I'd find that rainbow's neck and twist.
Remove any imperfect flickers, too-thick

clots of light, and slice. From end to end I'd skin
it, ripping colour, one from another, clean;

not letting indigo seep into violet; dividing
red from orange with a firm, Biblical hand.

I'd cut it into slices, wrap them up in paper,
feed you chunks of it, later, while we watched

the sky and chomped; vibrancy flooding our
happy mouths, miracle filling our throats.

Poem for the Lost Ones

Written after the murder of my aunt, who is referenced in the poem

O lost one, cruel heart,
I want to tell you that you are loved.
You, with the vestiges of sin
smeared around your greasy chin –
yes, you. I want to tell you
that there is a place where these things
do not matter; where all will be, finally,
forgiven. Yes, I am speaking to you,
sinner – you who stole the gold from
your mother's mouth, the warmth
of her final breath still rasping on your hand;
You who last night had your hand inside a till,
or foraging between the legs of a child.
Heartless, taker – I am telling you
that you are loved. That there is a love
which sees beyond the blood on your boot-heel
after you stamped that woman to death.
The alleyway you followed her down
was filled with love. You swam through it
like a fish caught in a stream. Rapist,
you have already been hooked.
Yes, there will be a judgement but it will not
come from this. This which in fact is everything:
the hand, the heart, the eye, the blade;
this which embraces you like a lost child;
which, in the end, will carry you home.

Sustenance

I know your body, now,
like the inside of my mouth.

Your skin has become
familiar as rain.

Your atoms fly to me
like honey bees, they

nestle in my hair;
nuzzle at my neck.

I breathe you in,
smooth you like paper.

Your face is my favourite
book, these days.

Your flesh is my food,
my water.

Words

After anger, your lips
are as soft and penitent
as the pears which droop
from that tree.

We lie together
on the warm, naked belly
of an afternoon, feasting
on each other.

It is enough to make me
want those words, so
hard and bitter,
again.

When

I think of you, I sink
so deeply into Love that
all the conkers of the world
slip spontaneously from their
shells; take off their spiky coats
like gangsters going to prayer;
ease themselves of every
sin and slide softly to the earth
where, brown and round and
Buddha-like, they shine.

Ascension

From inside unlit bulbs they climb,
feeling through the crumbling dark;
fearless spears, insistent shoots,
certain even in the dirt that there's
another world, *up there.*

Eating earth with hungry roots,
finding paths through stone and rock,
endlessly rising, eventually emerging,
green tongues poking from the ground
as if to say *I told you so.*

Advancing upwards, ever further,
reaching for their unknown goal;
finally unfurling, bursting into flower.
star-like, sun-cast, their golden glory
sings out: *even in the dark, we knew,*

that this is what we were.

Indigo Dreams Publishing Ltd
24, Forest Houses
Cookworthy Moor
Halwill
Beaworthy
Devon
EX21 5UU
www.indigodreams.co.uk